As I write this book on Thanksgiving Day

of 2023, I am very grateful to those who

have profoundly impacted my life.

This book is dedicated to them. First and

foremost, I express My love and gratitude
to my wife, Bonita, who has filled my life

with boundless love, honesty, friendship,
and understanding. I am grateful to my

mother, Earleene, and brother, Ivan, for

helping me after an accident. My brother

Vincent who showed me the technique,

my father Robert instilled life's virtue.

Thank You

Welcome and thank you for your interest

in my book and for being able to show

you a form of art that is exciting and

rewarding both mentally and

emotionally as well as relaxing. I am not

a professional, but I have been working
with various kinds of art all my life. Please
enjoy Thank You for trying

this Technique

Introduction

This book is designed for the beginner

who would like to show their creativity

and rewarding art form that allows the

transforming of ordinary glass surfaces,

mirrors, or glassware to be awesome

work of art.

This art form does not require you to be

an artist or someone who cannot draw.

You are able to get all of the free artwork

and or stencils needed to accomplish

such a rewarding feeling, one that would

make you excited enough to do another

and another.

This book has been written to express

the fun, exciting, and a beautiful way to

show your art and creativity with an

inexpensive way of expression.

Glass etching is a creative and rewarding

form of art that allows you to transform
a piece of ordinary glass or mirror

surfaces Into stunning works of art.

There are many different ways to etch

glass, but what I am referring to in this

book is a hand-held held inexpensive

Dremel tool to etch or engrave onto the

glass. This style of art to me is gratifying,

enjoyable, and relaxing.

Within just a few hours you will have a

masterpiece that you and others can

enjoy for a lifetime. Everyone has an

imagination, don't be afraid to use it.

You can create your artwork on many

different types of glass, windows, wood,

metal, automobile glass, house doors,

house windows, as well as glassware.

You are also able to make some

awesome gifts that you have made that

cannot be Found anywhere in the world

but are something special from you.

There are so many free art patterns on

the internet that can get you started, or

you can go to craft stores and purchase

different patterns to use.

This all depends on the artist and what

first.

Start with a simple design, transfer it

onto the back of a mirror or piece of glass,

and be amazed as your artwork comes to

life.

There will be extra information on how

to make an awesome art display for the

wall.

Information about the Author

My name is Bruce W Brewer and have

been blessed with the talent of drawing:

(Pencil, ink, etching, painting, and wood

carving).

I have spent my life of 60+ years, striving

to get better and be better as I go. Back

in 2010, I was in a bad accident that kept

me in a hospital for several days, then in

and out of therapy for several months.

My brother and mother gave me a place

to stay until I was released to go home,

which was approximately 600 miles
from my wife, and our little girl

(standard teacup chihuahua) Babette, and
my home.

Life has a way of picking you up and

letting you down, but the truth is, it is a

mindset.

You must learn how to control life in a

way that is more manageable, and I

found the way out of reality for a brief

period of time, by doing what I really

enjoy doing not because I must but

because I want to.

My youngest brother showed me what to

do and what I needed to do, but it was up

to me to figure out the way I felt most

comfortable with. This part of the

artwork world is considered trial and

error.

My first attempt was to freehand the

Harley-Davidson banner onto the back of

a mirror, etch it out, and my brother will

display it in his house.

I forgot that if you don't turn the letters

backward, when I turned the mirror

around, all the words were backward.

I thought I would fail (first attempt in

learning), but my brother said it was

awesome, so he framed it and placed it

on the wall in his restroom on the

opposite side of the mirror he used to

shave with.

Now he is able to look at the mirror the

way it was supposed to have turned out

originally.

Artwork has always been my passion

and I have a calming and relaxing way

about it. Your artwork will never be

perfect for you, but others will not

recognize anything wrong unless you

point it out.

Be proud of what you have done and

remember there is no such thing as

being a perfectionist because nothing

will ever be perfect, but it will be the best

that you can do, and the more you do it

the better you will get at it.

This is my first attempt at writing about

something that I have enjoyed doing,

having trial and error with the problem

of breaking a few mirrors because I

etched too deep into the glass, or set the

mirror on the floor so I could get myself

something to drink, and accidentally

rolled my chair into the mirror and

busted it into many pieces.

This was before I learned to place some

kind of shelving adhesive or even clear

wide tape on the mirror side of the

mirror, so whenever the glass cracks or

breaks, it would not send shards of

broken glass everywhere.

The clear adhesive tape or shelf liner will

allow you to see what your artwork

looks like when you turn the mirror so

you can see what was etched.

Not if but when you break one of your

masterpieces, you just do it again.

This is a learning experience, it is not like

it is not going to happen, but when will it

happen?

Do not get upset because it happens to

everyone at one point or another when

you etch mirrors.

It seems that when this happens, it will

make you more aware of how deep you

etch the glass, be aware of where you

place the mirror, and try to keep it from

happening again.

After this type of incident(s) happened,

the next etching seemed to be a better

piece of artwork than the one before, it is

because now you want to make sure this

does not happen again, soon.

This process is a comforting way to

embrace the talent deep inside of you.

This is my first book and would like to

teach others how I have learned to enjoy

what keeps me calm, stay focused and

relaxed from the world around me.

Do what you like doing best and show

your skills in a way no one would ever

dream of.

This is my artist getaway for expression

and displayed for everyone to see and

appreciate.

The more you practice etching glass or

mirrors, the more exciting you get and

the more of the artwork, you will show

others.

This is the beauty and artistic ability

others will see, this will start others

talking and bragging about such

beautiful works of art you have

produced.

When they start talking to family and

friends about what they have witnessed

with their own eyes. They will have

others wanting to know more, and

before long, you might have a side income

that will help pay for more material, pay a

bill, by gas or whatever you like, as you

learn a new skill and enjoy what is

relaxing, rewarding and it will place

you in a happier state of mind.

This book has been written to help guide

the beginner and to give them some

understanding of what is possible and to

have fun and learn a new skill.

From an artist, author, life coach &

mentor, to another artist.

I want to express my most inward

concern for your safety from me to you,

please be aware of the safety hazards

involved and be patient.

Your innermost talent that you have

been blessed with will help you enjoy and

have fun with this new and exciting way

of art that you are going to create.

But please protect yourself, and the

room around you. Thank you for your

time and interest. You can do this.

History of Glass Etching

Different types of glass etching have

been a technique that was used from back

in the Roman days.

A long time ago the artist knew how to

place different types of etching and

artwork on different surfaces of glass to

express the artist's ability to showcase

for others, the artist's true form of art.

From what I could find, the earliest

known forms of the etching of glass date

back to the Roman Empire.

As time went on the art of etching glass

became more popular around the 1500s,

when the artists learned how to transfer

their artwork onto glass surfaces.

Some of the process that was used

involves the application of acidic, caustic,

or abrasive substances to the surface of

the glass being etched to create the

design the artist is after.

When this first started this was done

after the glass was blown or cast by the

glass makers also known as blown glass.

But there was another form of etching

that has taken place, and it is mold

etching that will in time replace some of

the glass etching.

This happened back at the beginning of

the new error when this time in the

century was starting to really get

involved with their art ability.

Glass etching is when you remove

minute mounts or small amounts of

glass, causing the characteristics of a

rough surface and the translucent quality

of a frosted glass.

During the Roman Empire Period, glass

was used as tableware or as containers

or vessels used for expensive oils,

perfumes, and medicines.

This method of etching was called wheel

cutting, where the artist would take a

piece of glass and rotate it against a

metal wheel with abrasives.

The Romans also used a method called

cameo glass, in which the artist would

take two or more colored pieces of glass,

fuse them together then etch off the

upper layer revealing the lower layers

that created a contrast between colors

and it was called the relief effect.

The Roman glass industry sprang from

almost nothing and developed to full

maturity over a couple of generations

during the first half of the first century

A.D.

Since Rome was the dominant political,

military, and economic power in the

Mediterranean world, it was a major

factor in attracting skilled craftsmen to

set up workshops in the city.

Core-formed and cast glass vessels were

first produced in Egypt and

Mesopotamia as early as the fifteenth

century B.C., but only began to be

imported and, to a lesser extent, made on

the Italian peninsula in the mid-first

millennium B.C.

In the 1800s, the English glasshouses

continued their production of deeply cut

crystal; engraved glass and started the

process of coloring and painting the

glass was given the greatest attention in

central Europe.

The Venetian glasshouses at Murano

were the leading houses or businesses of

etched glass.

Core-formed and cast glass vessels were

first produced in Egypt and

Mesopotamia as early as the fifteenth

century B.C., but only began to be

imported and, to a lesser

extent, made on the Italian peninsula in

the mid-first millennium B.C.

By the 21st century, glass etching is still

popular as a form of art, a hobby, and a

craft that artists are enjoying today.

Different Techniques

Glass and Mirror etching

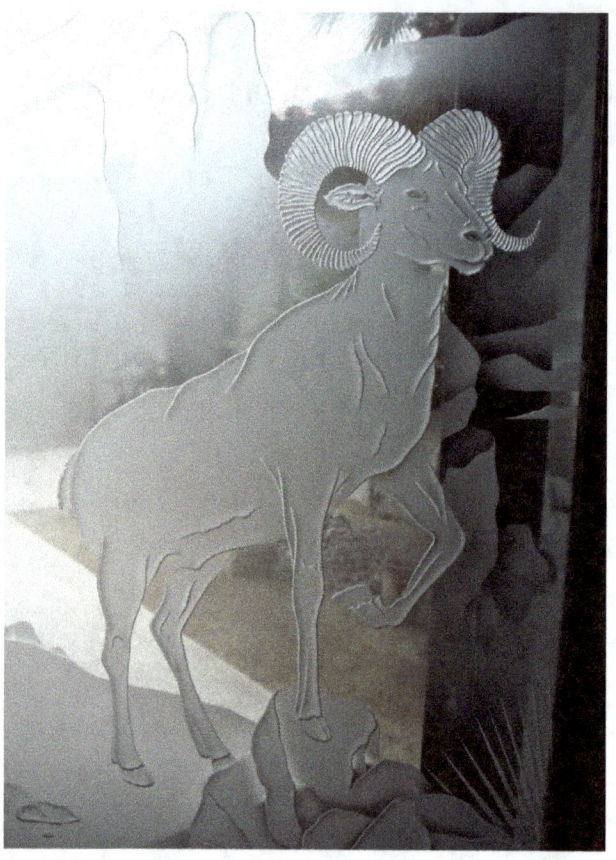

The picture of this ram shows the

different aspects of the depth that will

show up on the opposite side of the

mirror or glass when it is turned around.

Remember to trace the outlines first

then add the shading which looks like

the frosted glass in the picture.

The parts of the ram that looks frosted

are from just scratching the surface and

the other lines are parts of the mirror

that the artist did not etch and some of

the other lines are the highlighted edges

of the shadow.

Acid Etching:

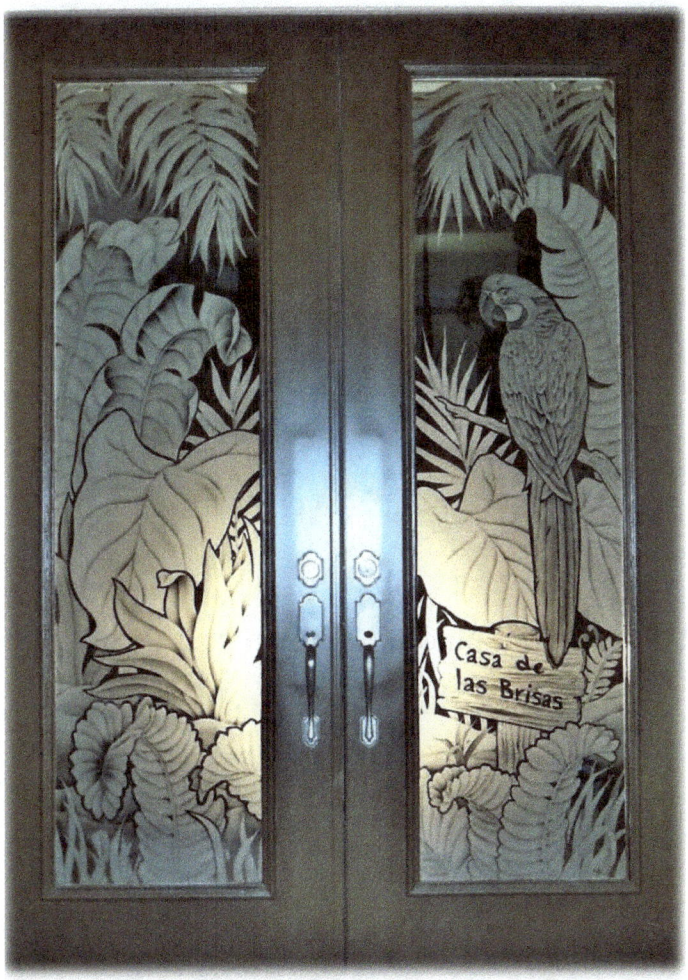

Casa de las Brisas

Acid etching is another form of using

chemicals. Acid etching is using

chemicals to accomplish the task of

etching the glass.

This process calls for several types of

safety equipment as well as a very well-

ventilated place to apply the acid.

This same artwork can be done with a

Dremel tool if you want to take the time.

The outcome is beautiful, and you are

able to use the stained-glass paint and

make these drawings are very colorful.

Sandblasting:

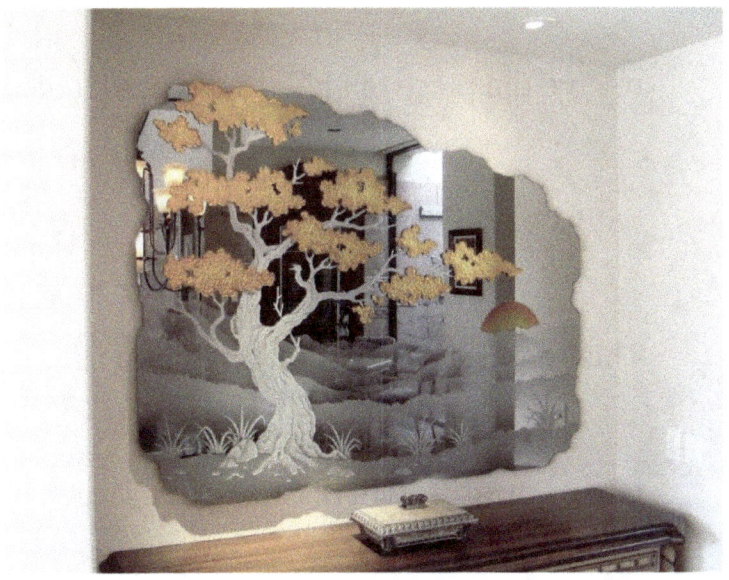

Sandblasting is another way of etching

mirrors or glass. It uses compressed air

and varied sizes of sand beads or glass

beads that artists can use in the same

sandblasting gun to spray onto the glass

to give the piece of glass the frosted look

with a pattern in place.

This requires ventilation, in a shop

where the dust will dissipate in a larger

area.

This artist cut the mirror into a unique shape. This artist has added minimal amount of paint to accent the drawing.

I have found in different mom-and-pop shops, I have found different unique mirrors that have different shapes you can purchase and use for your artwork.

Laser Etching:

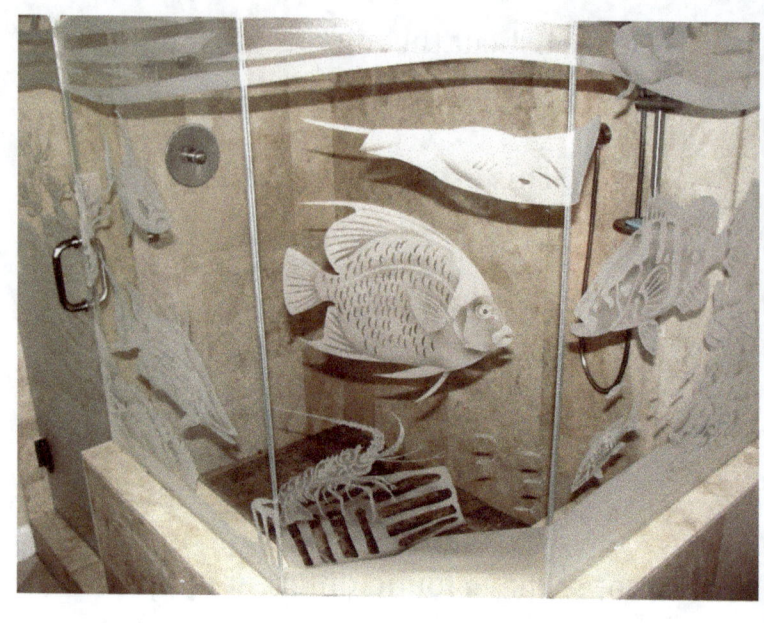

Laser etching is another awesome way

to make beautiful artwork on larger

surfaces. This process uses a beam of

light to create precise and detailed

designs on the glass.

This process takes more room and

takes special equipment to produce this

kind of artwork.

There is no limit to what can be

accomplished with your artwork, no

matter what means of etching you want

to use.

Experiment and have fun, whether it is

for a bathroom shower glass, a bathroom

mirror, or a dining room display.

All etching artworks can be

accomplished in many forms, but all of

these pictures or drawings can be

accomplished with handheld Dremel

tools.

Tools

Tools: For the several types of etchings:

- Dremel or Cordless Engraving Pen with Diamond Bits
-
- Glass etching cream and application brushes
-
- Aluminum Oxide, Sand (80, 100, or 120 grit), glass beads, sand blaster gun for air
-
- compressor.
-
- Laser Engraver

For this book, the tools and material we will be using:

- A comfortable chair
-

- I use a TV tray or a table to be comfortable at

-

- Dremel Tool or Cordless Engraving Pen

-

- Diamond bits to etch the glass

-

- Artwork or Stencils

-

- Pencil

-

- Sharp knife maybe an exacto knife

-

- Pencil, to trace out the artwork onto the mirror or glass

-

- Ruler, to center the drawings on to the mirror or glass

-

- Scotch Tape, to hold the carbon paper and the drawing onto the glass

-

- Cleaner for the glass, lint-free cloth, or rag for wiping off the glass

-
- Foam Brush, to brush off excess shavings
-
- Carbon Paper, to transfer the artwork on the mirror, or draw on the glass
-
- Adhesive paper, to place on the mirror side of the mirror for protection
-
- Box of 12 x 12 mirrors, to be etched on
-
- Artwork to be etched
-
- Plexiglas, for the protection of your artwork within the shadow box
-
- Hangers for the artwork or a safe place until you display it.
-
- Shadow box, for the mirror and same size Plexiglas to be placed into.

-
- Small battery-powered Christmas lights, clear if the artwork is painted or colored
-
- if color has not been added, (your choice depends on if your artwork has been
-
- painted).
-
- Some kind of glue, preferably hot glue, to hold the lights inside of the shadow box.

When you have gathered all the tools

needed to start, find the piece of

artwork, draw your piece of artwork, or

download and print the design that you

really like and want to make an etch of,

possibly found on the internet.

You will have to start somewhere, and

once you start, you will lose a sense of

time and enjoy the process so

much, that you cannot wait to try

another and another and another.

Have fun, enjoy the gifts GOD has blessed

you with, and now that you have

accomplished what you feared the most

is now going to be your next most

beautiful piece of artwork.

Take pictures, sign, and date, then

display for all to see.

Art Inspirations

Wildlife Animals:

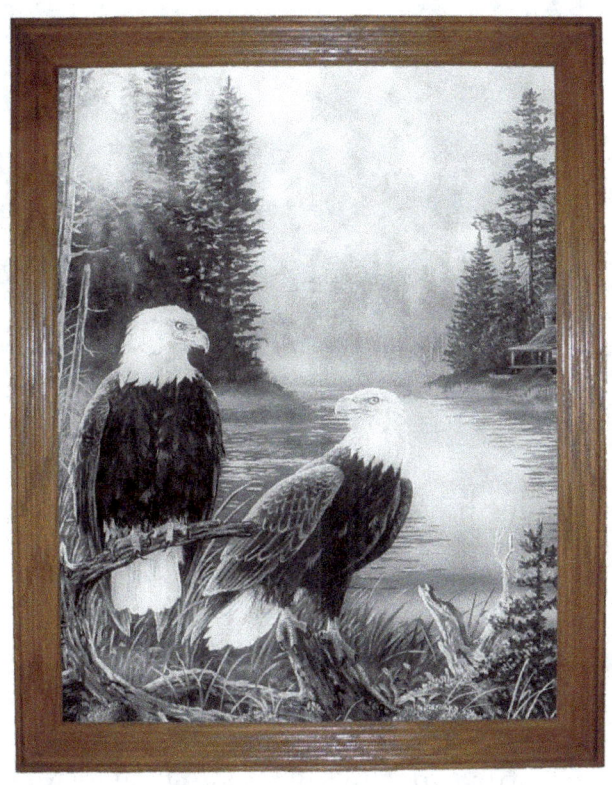

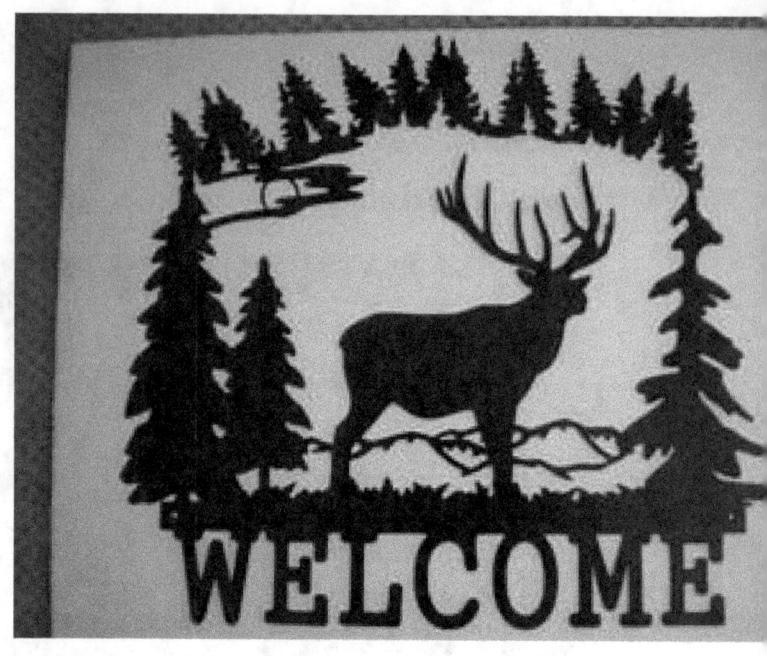

Eagles have always been my weakness

as far as watching these amazing

creatures in the wild as well as drawing

and etching them.

The deer and elk play a special place in

hunters, and people who enjoy watching

the beautiful nature all around us. Do not

be afraid of what is possible in the art

world of creation. You each have a mind

of your own, know what your tastes are,

and have a love of accomplishment

whenever it comes from inside of you.

There is more of this beautiful nature

that is waiting to be captured from an

artist's perspective and on how the artist

would like to tell their story on the

etchings created.

Remember this artwork is how you see it

from your eyes, not from what someone

else envisions, unless you are working

on this piece of artwork for someone
else, and you would like to make it the

best it can be.

Everyone will see it differently with their

own eyes. Being different is how to

display what you want to see and be

proud to say you did this.

Wildlife Animal Etching Continued:

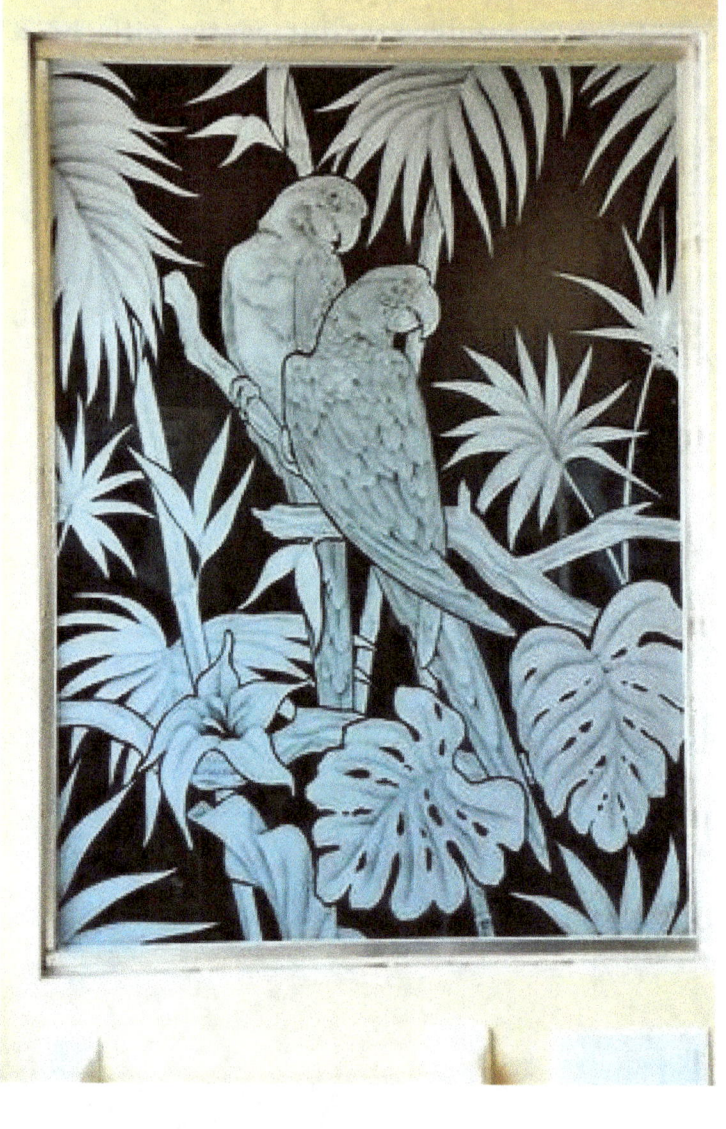

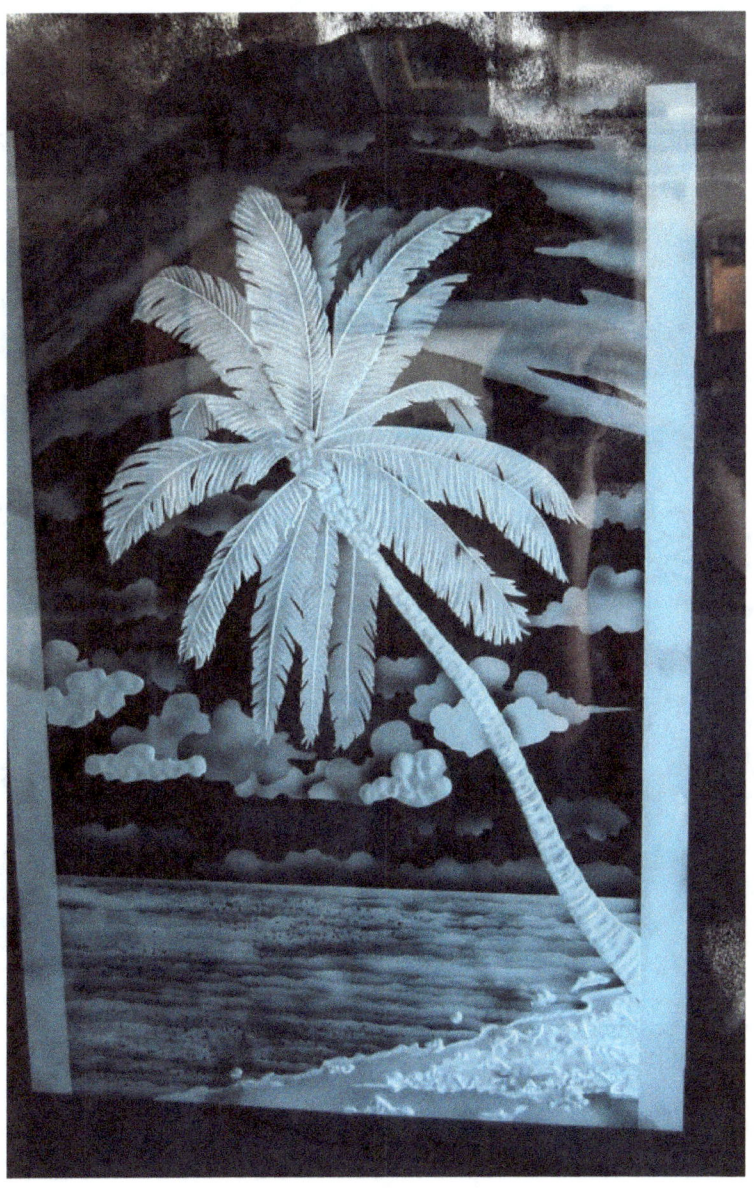

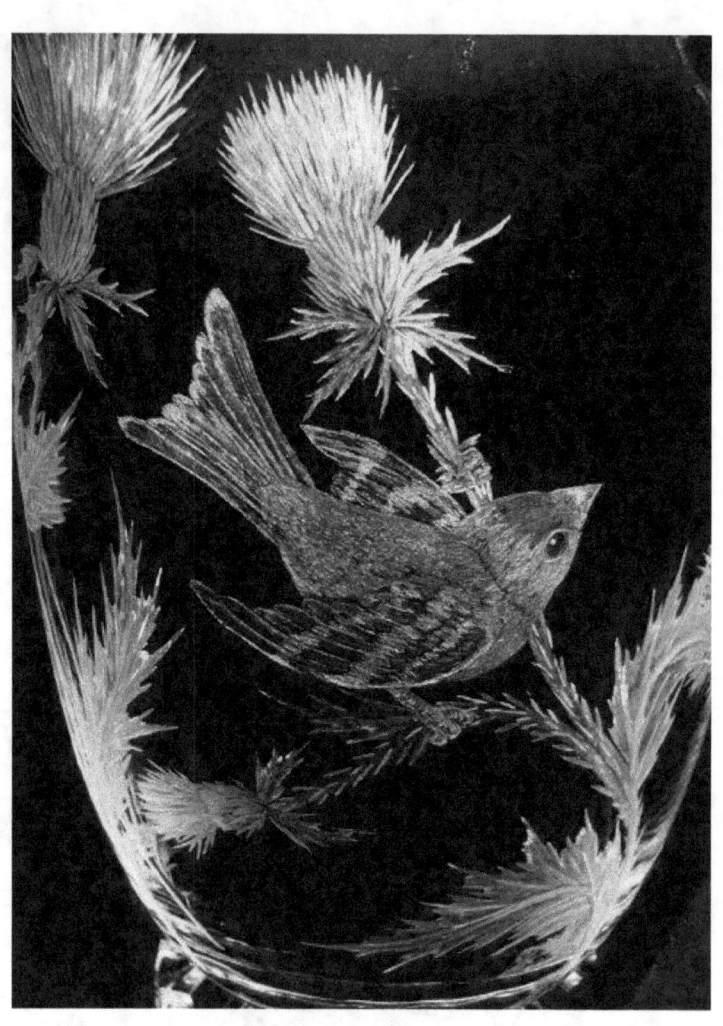

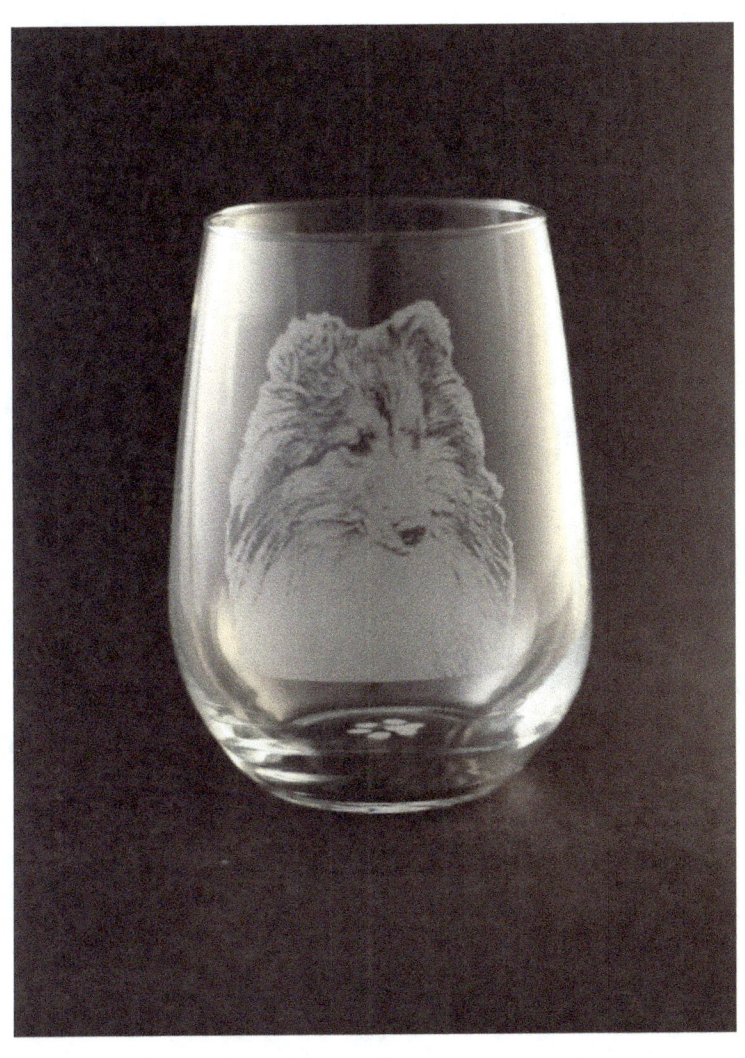

All these pictures have been etched and

some of them added color to, but it is not

necessary. You are not limited to what

you can etch on. Animals that have

been introduced into our lives, are

awesome ways to display your artwork

that the customer will appreciate it for

years to come. No one else would have

what you have created.

These are some of my favorites. When

others see what is possible with your

creations, you might be asked to make a

time capsule of a mirror for individuals

in love, past loved ones, artwork that has

never been seen by anyone but you, or

artwork that someone else has asked

you to do.

These pictures are some ideas for you to

begin your journey, but the internet has

so much more to offer for the artist's

imagination.

Before you start getting crazy:

Remember that practice helps you to

understand what will and will not work

for you but puts you in a position that

will allow you to be able to etch on any

medium, at anytime, anywhere.

Flowers and Plants:

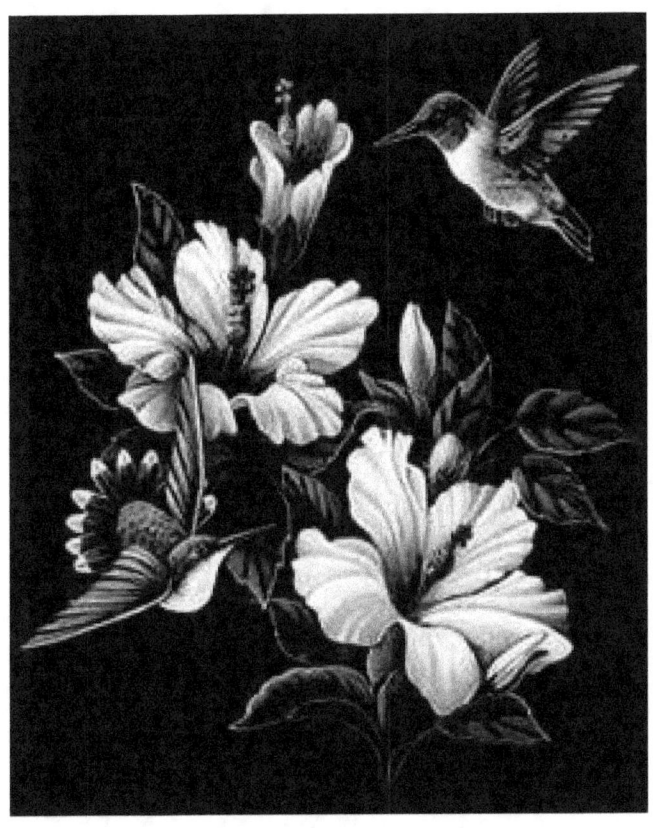

This picture is used for my cover page.

Memories of my wife and all of her

beautiful plants with the hummingbirds

playing and feeding, what an amazing

site.

I found animals and plants to be an

awesome way to express God's awesome

creations. People that love nature and all

that it has to offer would love to see

pictures like this.

Pick the pictures or artwork that might

make you think it is too challenging, and

if so, start with a simpler design that you

would like to start with.

Find one you really like which will make

the learning processes are a lot more

enjoyable.

It really doesn't matter what you want to

place on a piece of glass, mirror, or

glassware, you can accomplish any

one of these tasks if you do not get in a

hurry.

Stay focused on the lines you are getting

ready to etch. When and if needed, get

kind of magnification to get a closer look

at your artwork and understand how the

different depths of etching cause a lot of

different effects that you will be able to

see, and manipulate, and as you go you

will be getting more precise on the

etching of your artwork.

Automobiles:

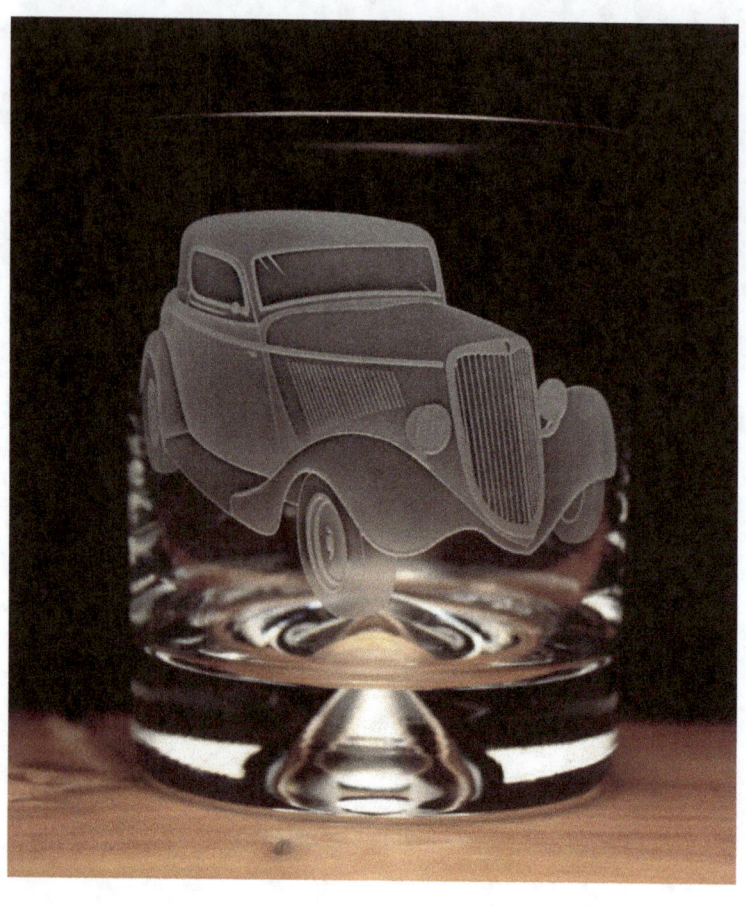

The artwork of old cars has always been my passion. Growing up, I admired all of

the old automobiles that were from the

past, because of my upbringing, my

father and brother have always worked

on and owned older automobiles. But the

style and customization of the art aspects

of the automobile, as well as the chrome

and the body style set the old automobile

apart from all the other vehicles ever

made.

They had a style that is not copied today.

This type of etching would go across and

sell very well at car shows, with all of the

different types of cars, trucks, pickups,

motorcycles, campers, the list goes on

and on.

This artwork can be displayed with

drinking glasses, mirrors, or anything

else you might have etched that would

bring you a pretty dollar if that were what

you are looking to do.

Aquatic Life:

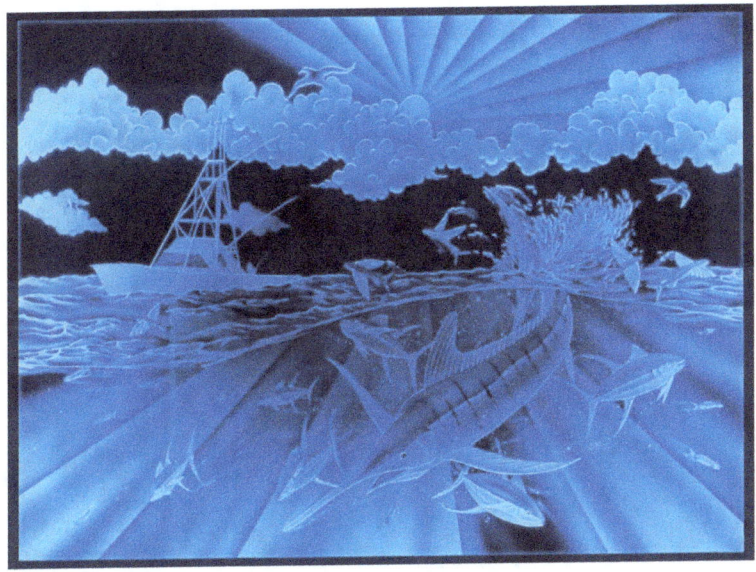

Sea Life, Boat & the Sky, what beautiful

etching. Being born under a water sign, I

am drawn to the water, the outdoors,

and all the wildlife that GOD has created.

If you enjoy the world around you, look

at all that nature has to offer.

Most of these pictures are from

someone's imagination who was able to

etch onto a piece of glass. This is how

you will learn to create different shadows

and images with the different techniques

and depths of etching that allow you to

have a more unique etching.

Wake up before the sun comes up or go

down and grab a window seat that will

never be copied again, unless you take a

picture and produce a piece of artwork

from the artist's eye of creation.

Names and Dates:

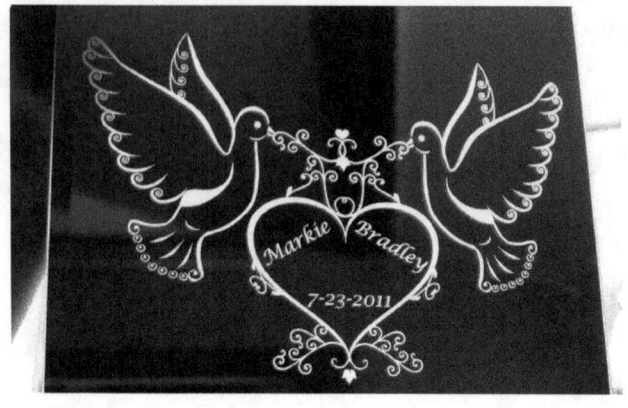

This can be done for any occasion.

Something as simple as this can make a beautiful art hanging that will be

admired for years, signifying the love and the date of togetherness for memories.

This kind of artwork is seen on the back

glass of cars and trucks, memories of the

past love and the memory of family and

friends. Be open to suggestions from

family and friends on their input from

you're drawing before etching.

Everything you see in white is where the

mirror has been etched.

Boats:

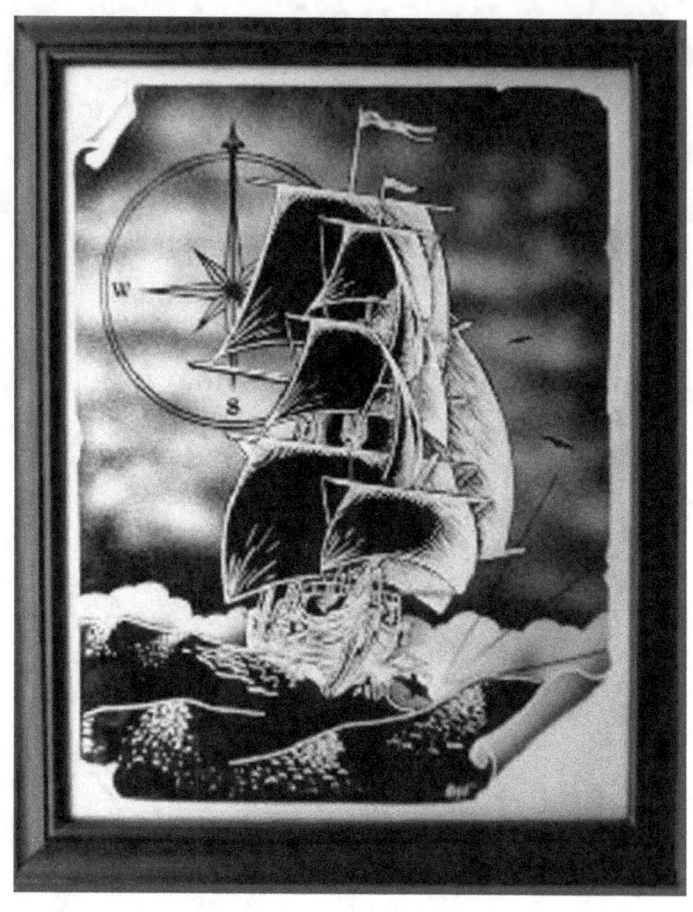

When I wanted to add a boat to my book,

I have always liked the old ships from

the days past. The style and beauty that

the builders back then had accomplished

with so little compared to what we have

today.

Most captains of any type of sea vessel,

whether it is a Pirogue a flat bottom

boat, v-bottom boat, tunnel bottom boat,

racing boat, houseboat, fishing boat,

shrimp boat, or any vessel that has sailed

the waters by river, lake, bay, or ocean.

The reason behind the captains wanting

the picture is that I have worked on the

shrimp boats, Offshore work boats, and

own flat bottom boats, but most of all,

love to see, admire, and sketch some of

these amazing vessels.

Would be proud to display the work of

art displaying something they have given

their life to do or enjoy doing. No one can

take this away from them, EVER.

Cartoons:

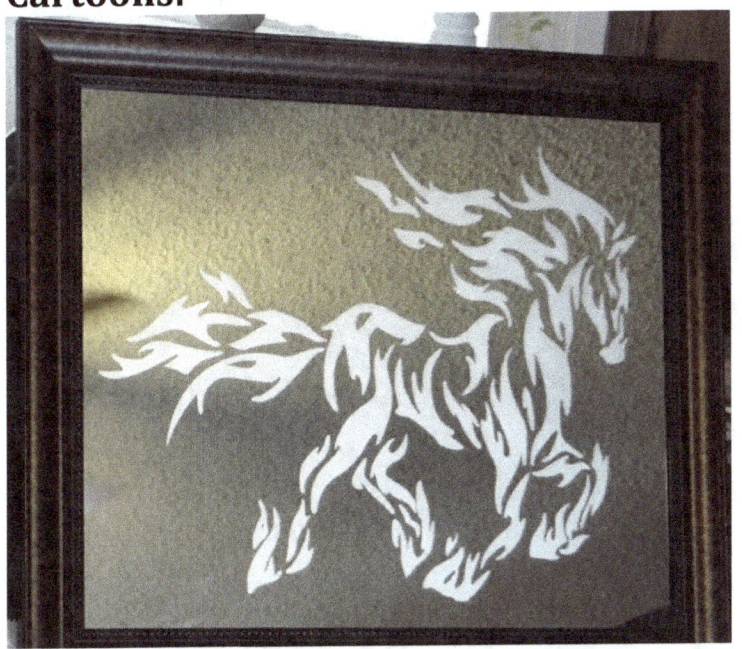

I found an etching of a piece of artwork

of a flaming horse and thought it would

be an interesting display of an artist's

imagination. The sky is the limit to what

you would be able to accomplish.

You can create and display anything; but

to sell your etchings, it must be

original, or something the customer has

ordered and is not copyrighted.

Bring your artistic ability out and be

proud of what you will be able to

accomplish with enjoyment and

understanding.

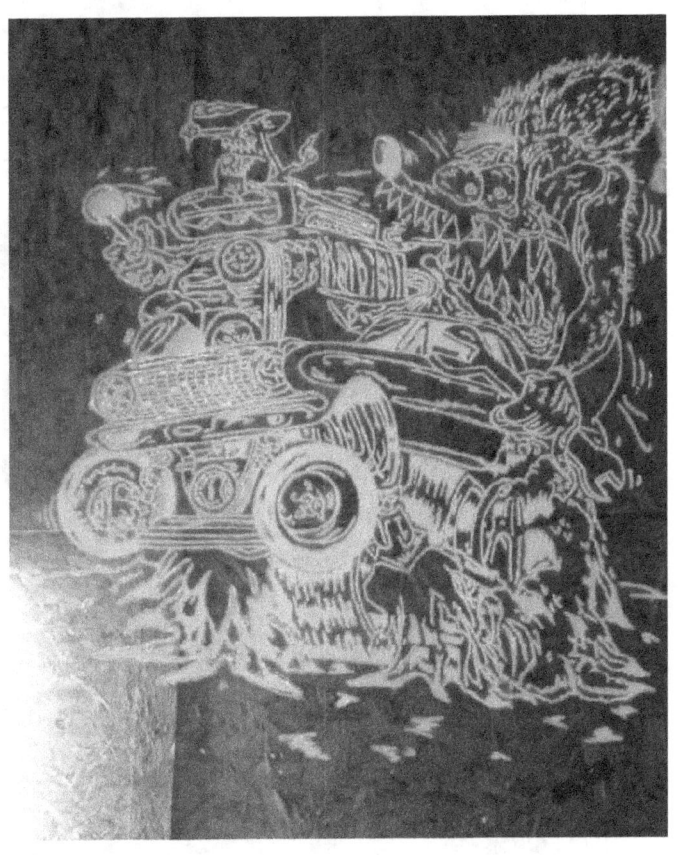

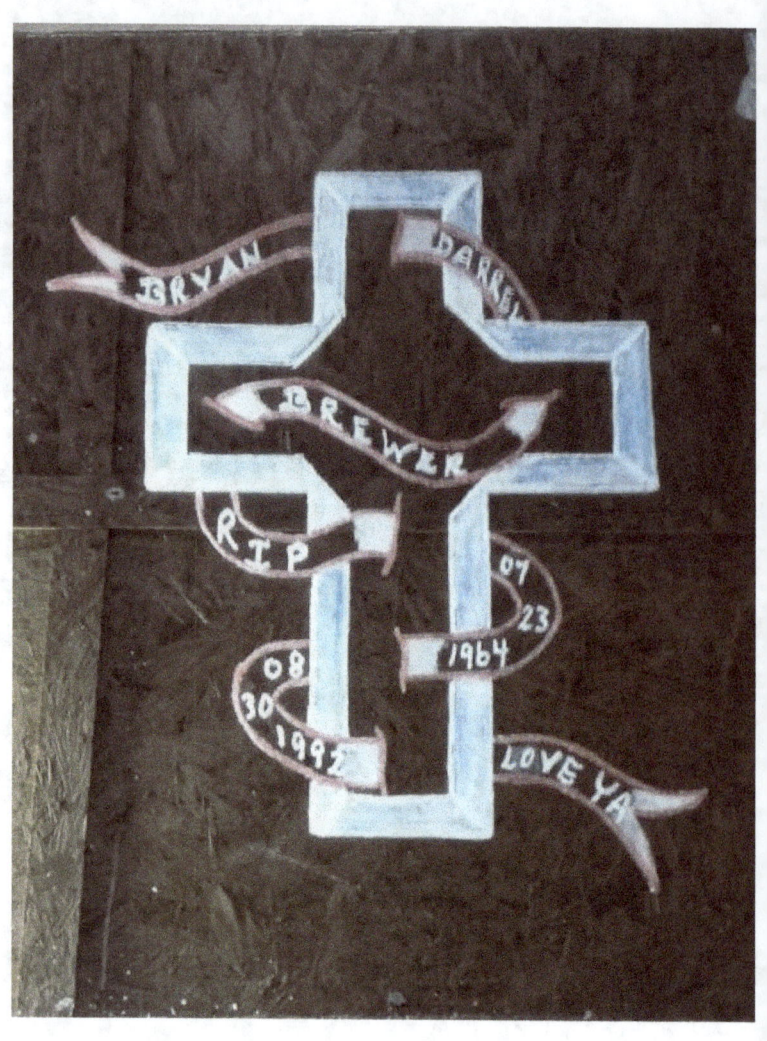

Self-created Art:

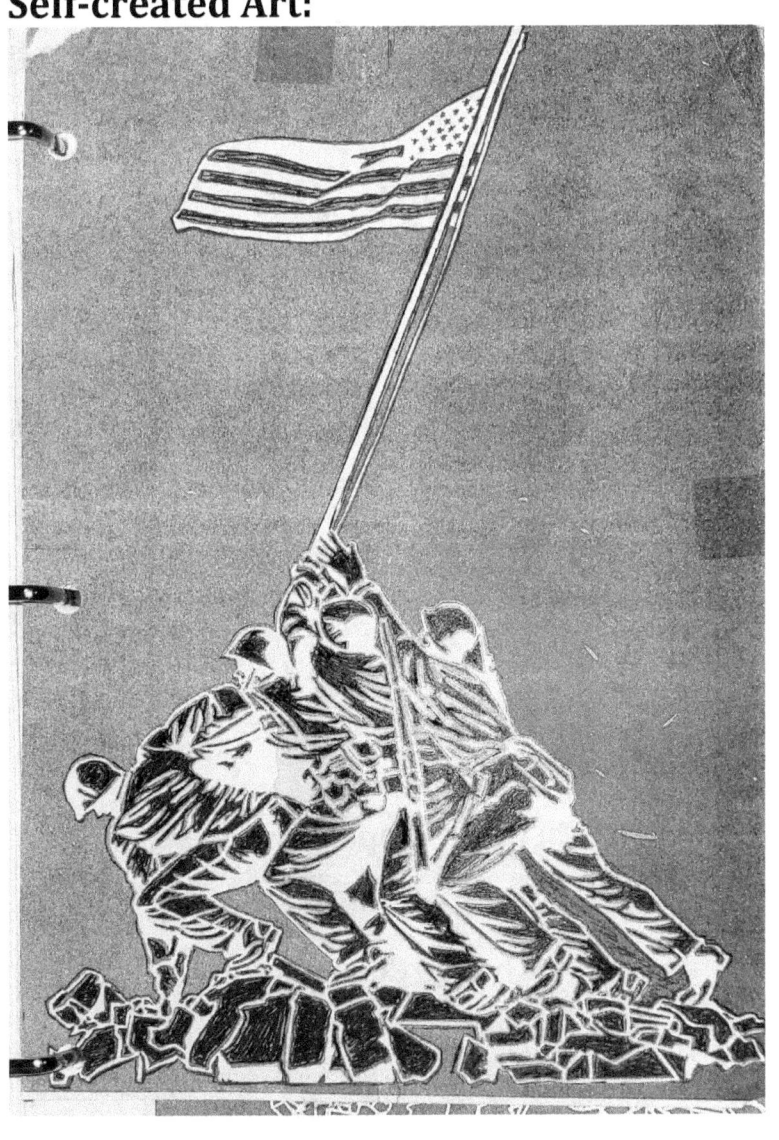

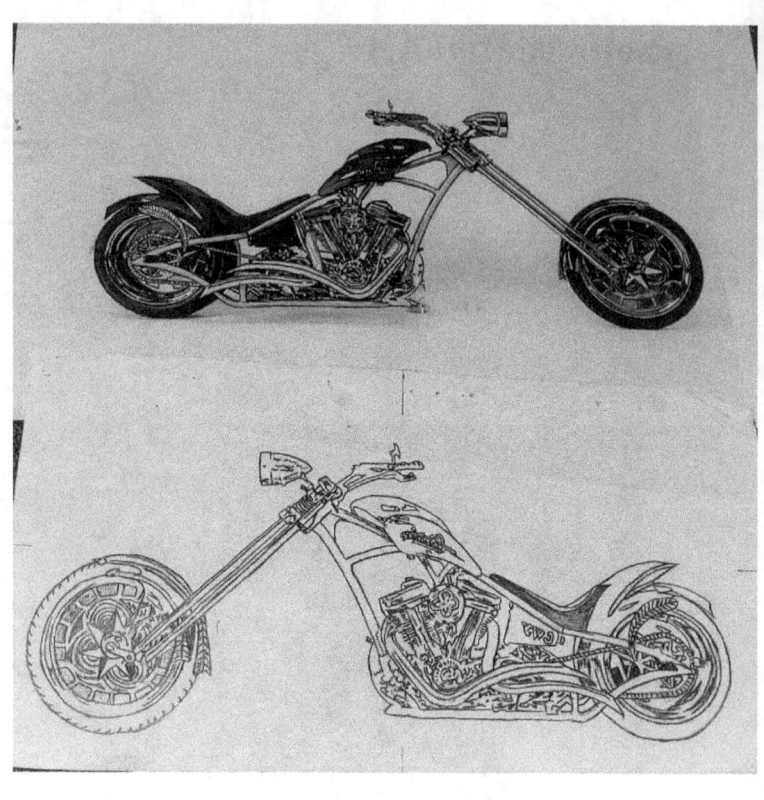

The Cherokee chopper was designed and

built by Orange County Chopper. I

personally, knew the owner of the bike.

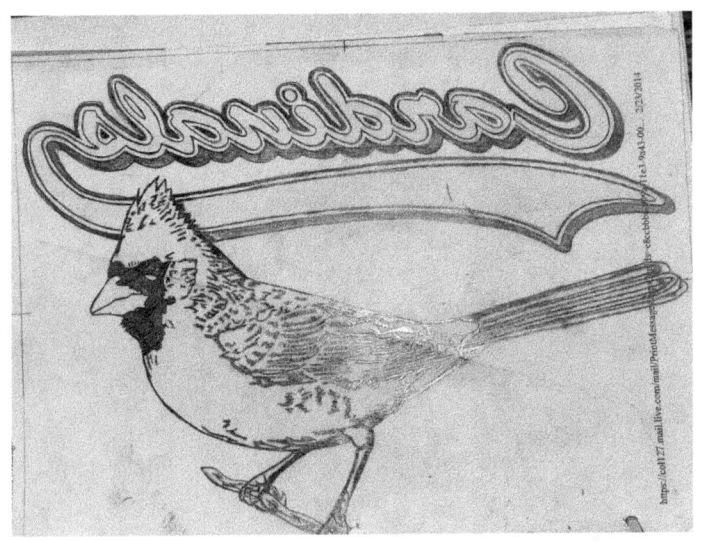

The cardinal is a very beautifully colored

bird, especially with their bright colors in

the snow. What an amazing animal to

Etch.

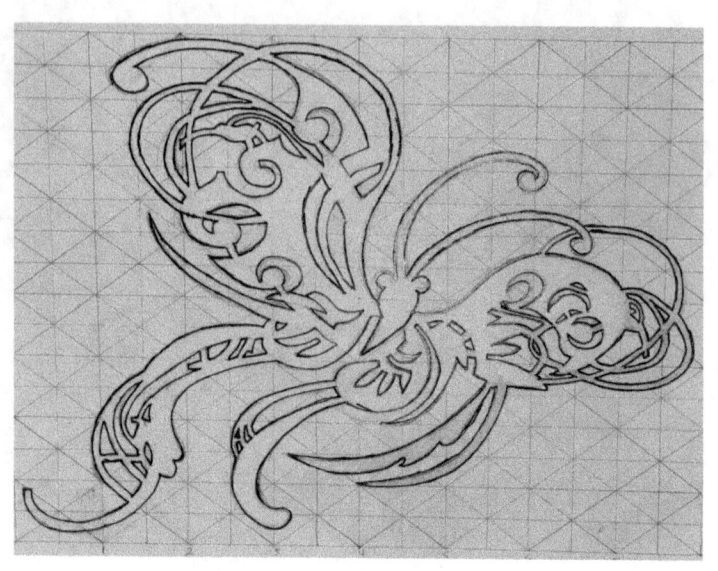

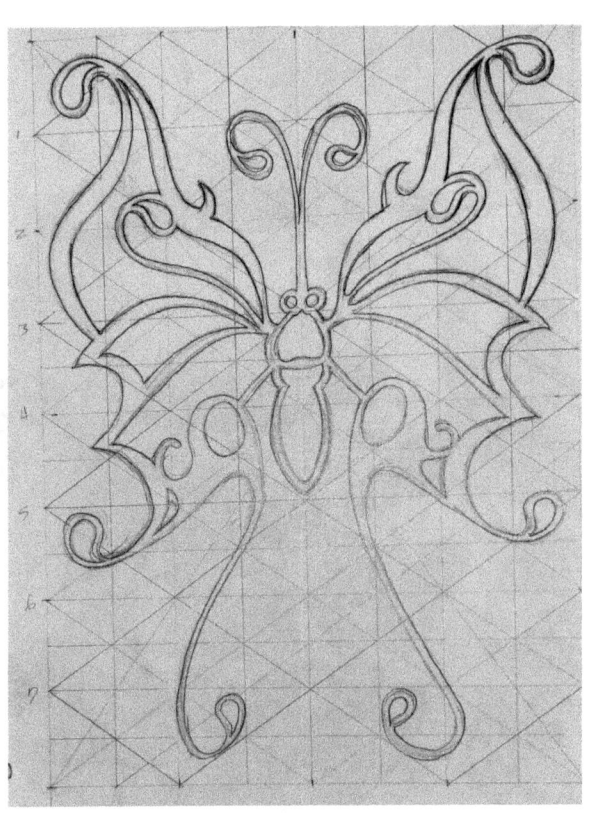

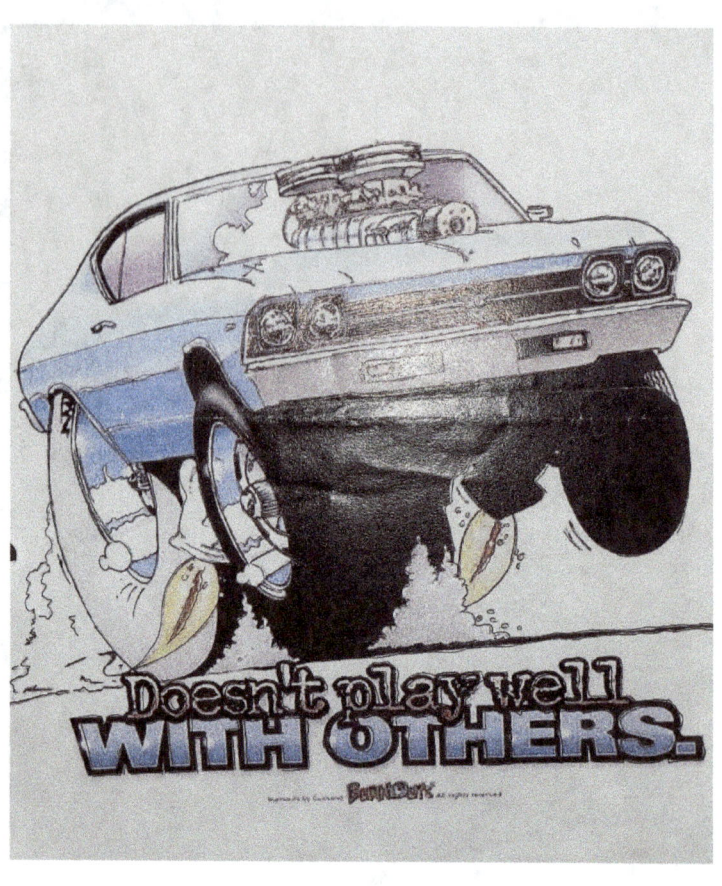

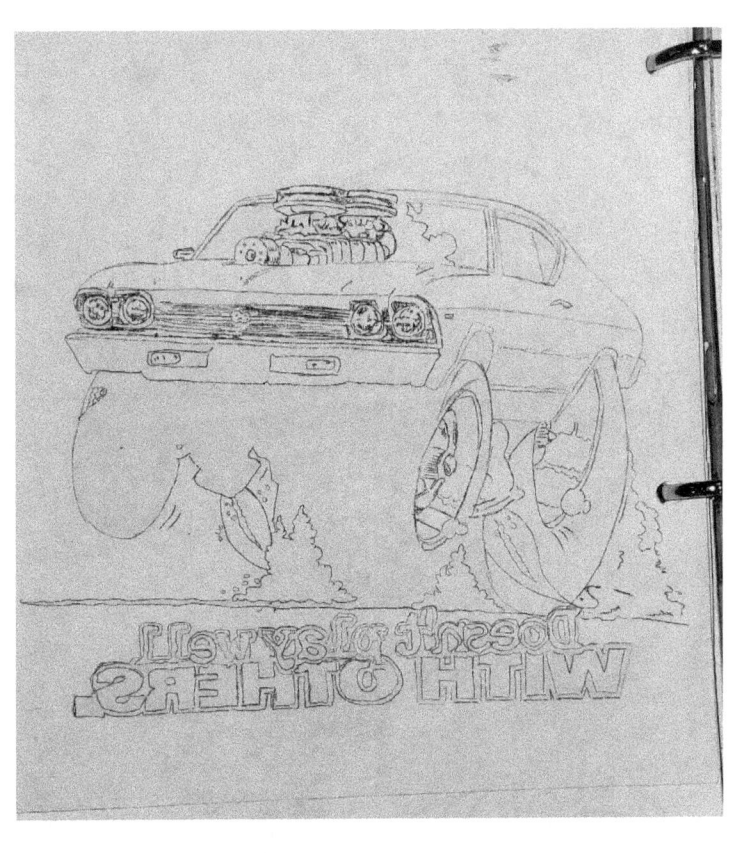

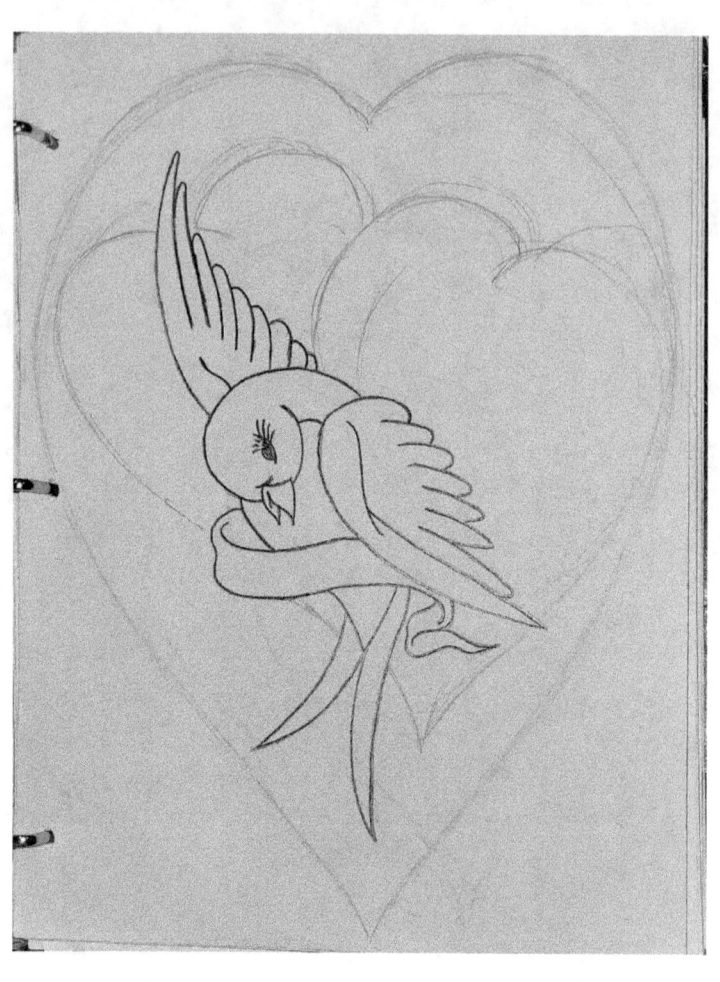

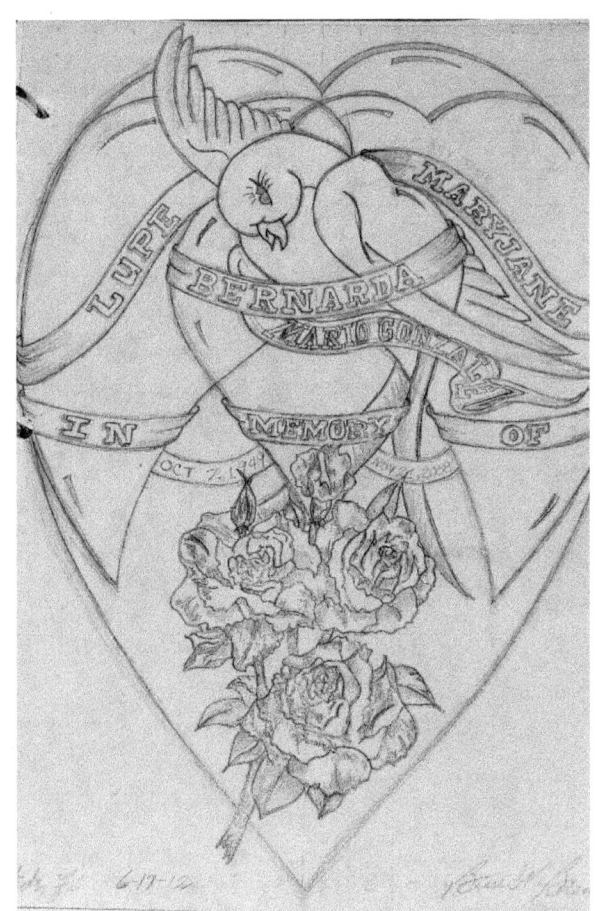

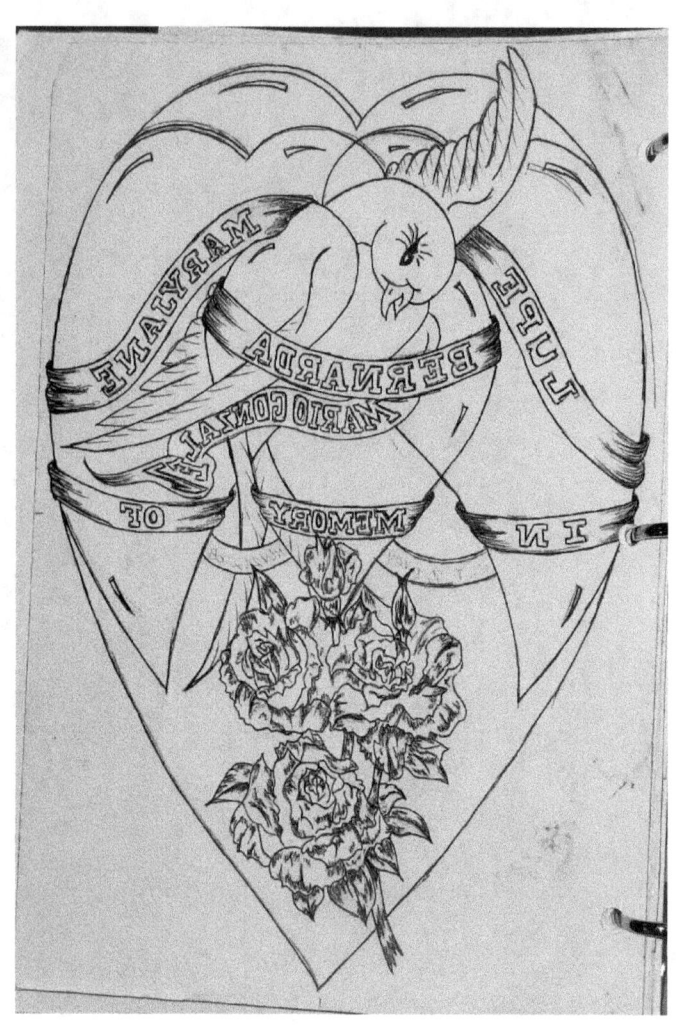

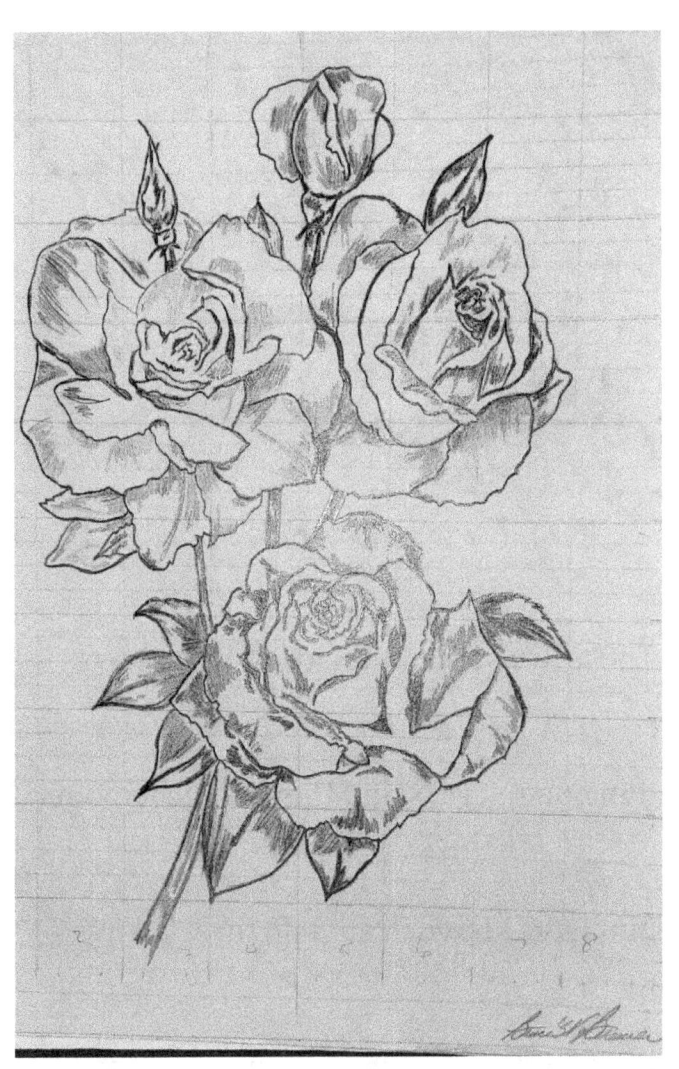

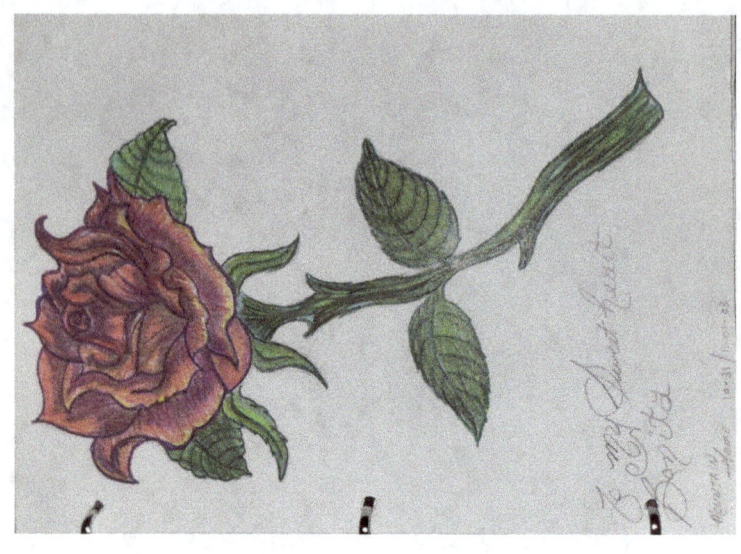

These are some of the drawings I have

done on mirrors and they all turned out

fantastic. I have drawn pictures all my

life and loved to show them off. Some of

these pictures were self-created and some of

them were made for the family, not for sale.

Whenever you start to store your artwork I

found that a 3-ring binder or some kind of

folder is best to store all my artwork in.

Take time to go back years later and reminisce

(look back) at all your accomplishments from the

past to now and see how you have progressed.

Etching the glass or mirrors is something that

cannot be erased. it is permanent.

Remember: Drawings and stencils can be used

repeatedly over and over again.

Tips: You can download free templates to get

started, and purchase some stencils at a craft

store or order the templates you would like to

create on glass.

Some of these drawings that are coming up are

free drawings that have been taken off the

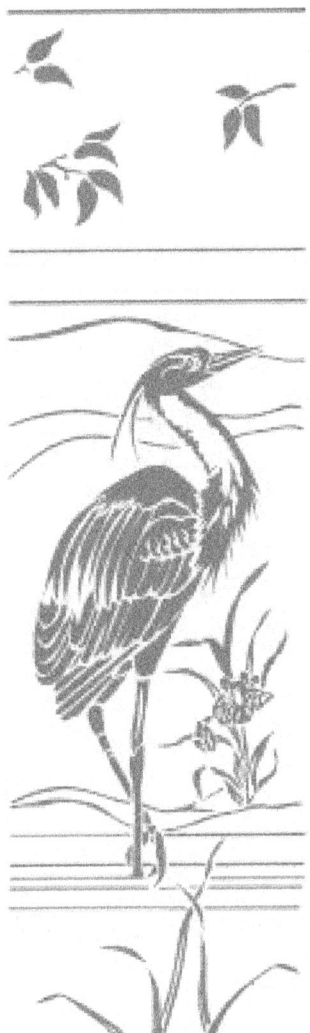

internet:

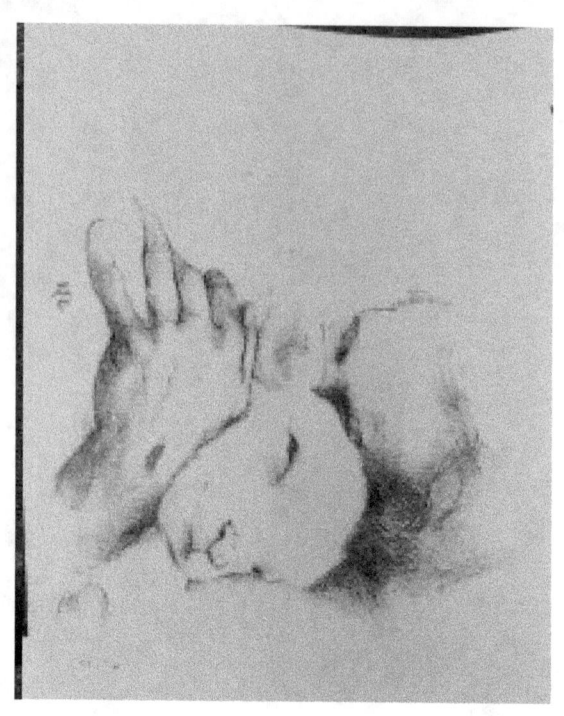

Some of these pictures I already have

printed out and are free pictures from

many years ago. Please excuse the way

some of these pictures are taken, I took

them at 4:00 a.m. and I did not realize

that the artwork was not cut out of the

picture.

I have been astounded by how many free

sketches, templates, and informational

videos are on this subject.

Whenever I etch, carve, draw, or paint

anything, I will always put a date and my

initials as to when this piece of art was

completed by me.

It makes a big difference to see not just

what you have accomplished, but the

pride and enjoyment you can take away

from this.

Step-by-step instructions:

1. Use a clean dry cloth, and wipe the mirror off on the front and back to get any lint, smudges, or fingerprints off the glass
2. Take adhesive paper and place it on the mirror side of the mirror to help protect the glass as you are turning and etching.
3. TIP: (I like to use a table place mat under the glass for easier turning and so as not to scratch the glass).
4. Turn the mirror or glass over onto the placemat. Take a ruler and mark the center on the edges of the mirror to line up the drawing you will be etching
5. Mark the center on the edges of the artwork that will be etched. Place the center marks on the artwork to the center marks on the mirror and place a piece of scotch tape on one end of the artwork onto the mirror.

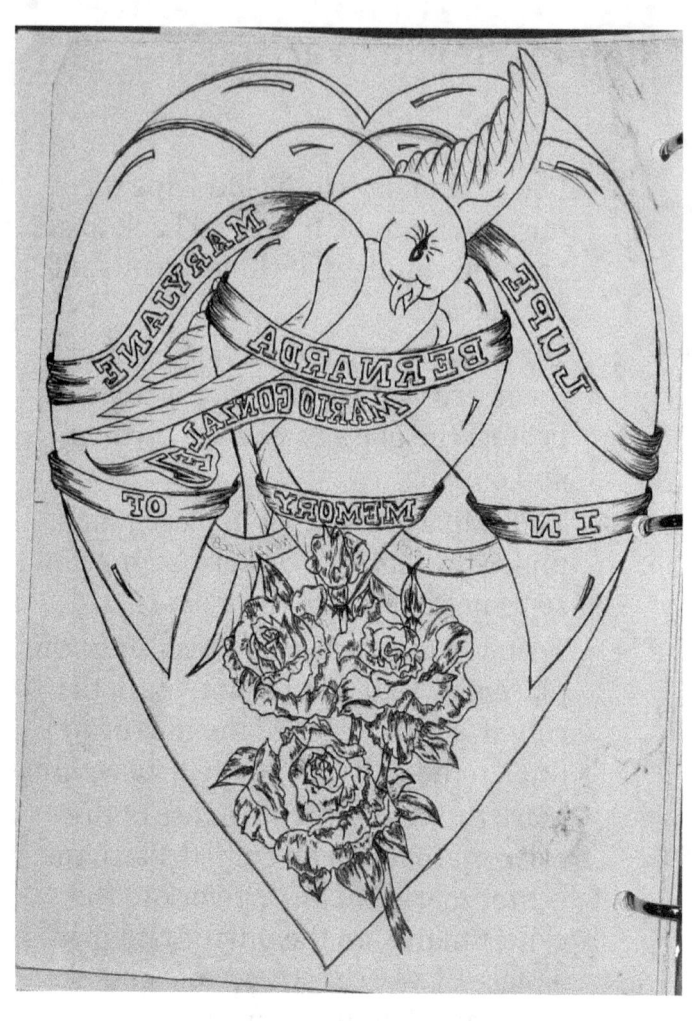

If you look on the page, you can see the

center marks lined up. This picture of

the doves also have footprints in the

sand etched on the other half of the

mirror for the ladies whose father has left

this world.

Take a piece of carbon paper with the

ink facing the mirror, and place the

carbon paper between the artwork and

the mirror. Secure the bottom edge with

another piece of scotch tape.

TIP: Remember, anything transferred

onto the mirror from the back will be

backward whenever you turn the mirror

around.

If the artwork needs to be reversed, you

could take the carbon paper and turn the

ink facing the backside of the artwork.

Now you can take a pencil and draw or

trace over your drawing and with the

carbon paper behind the artwork, your

artwork will be transferred to the back

and all you must do is

turn the artwork over and secure the

new drawing to the mirror (which will
be backward)

After you think you have traced all the

lines, undo the tape at the bottom of the

picture and the carbon paper, and make

sure to inspect all the lines that you

want to etch first before you start etching

the shadows.

This saves a lot of time, and since the

carbon paper is still attached to the top,

you will be able to line up the drawing

again, to continue where you might have

left off.

After the new piece of artwork has been

secured to the backside of the mirror,

start the tracing process over the

artwork for it to be transferred to the

mirror or glass.

When you think you are finished tracing

the artwork, lift the bottom of the

artwork, by taking the bottom piece of

tape up to reveal what has been

transferred to the glass.

Here is where you can tell if everything

needed has been traced and nothing is

missing, if you are missing a couple of

lines: you are still able to line up what

you already have as long as you don't

remove the top piece of tape until you are

sure, you have traced everything.

Take the artwork, carbon paper, and the

scotch tape off the back of the mirror.

Now it is time to start etching the outline

of the drawing.

TIPS: It would be a good idea if you took

a piece of paper and covered parts of the

artwork that will not be worked on at the

time so as not to smear the ink, it also

helps if a paper towel is placed under the

part of your hand that rests on the mirror

when etching.

Be sure to just scratch the surface of the
the backside of the glass so you will be

able to see the artwork coming to life.

After you have completed etching the

outline and make sure you have etched

all the artwork, you can now take the

artwork and the carbon paper off the

mirror.

It is time to start having some fun.

Remember the mirror and or glass is

only so thick, and if you etch too deep,

the glass will break, and you will have to

start over again. The deeper you etch into

the glass the different shading results you

will have on the mirror.

Experiment and have some fun. If you

use clear adhesive paper for the front of

the mirror, you will be able to turn the

mirror over and visually see the outcome

you are making on the mirror.

The adhesive tape is so if the mirror

cracks, chips, or breaks, you can

control where the glass is not going to

go.

When I am etching, I use a pair of

magnifying glasses to get a closer look at

the lines I am getting ready to etch.

Be sure to use your foam brush to brush

off the excess glass dust, or in a small

vacuum you can suck up the mirror dust

as you go.

After all of your artwork has been

transferred to the glass, you are almost

ready to showcase it.

If you would like to put color into your

picture, you can purchase a permanent

see-through stained-glass paint. You will

be able to place the paint onto where the

etching of the glass has taken place.

Now you will need a way to display your

artwork to keep it from getting damaged.

You can purchase just a frame, or you

can make or have made a shadow box.

EXTRA INFORMATION ON AN AWESOME DISPLAY FOR YOUR ARTWORK

When the shadow box is being made,

please make sure that you will have 2

slots at the front of the box.

The first is for a piece of Plexiglas the

same size as the mirror, and the second

is ½ an inch from the Plexiglas for the

mirror to be placed and protected from

flying debris.

Now you need a slot on the back for a

piece of fiberboard to house the battery

pack for the lights and as a backing to

house the lights.

This is just a picture of a shadow box

without the slots for the glass and

Plexiglas for protection.

After the shadow box has been built, and

the Plexiglas and the mirror have been

put into place, it is time to turn over the

shadow box, take your hot glue, and start

to glue the lights to the sides of the

shadow box behind the mirror.

Now cut a hole into the fiber board for

the battery pack of the lights to be

attached flush with the back side of the

shadow box. Now you can turn on or off

your lights.

Attach the fiberboard onto the shadow

box for completion.

Now for the reveal, turn the lights on and

turn the shadow box around.

Everywhere the mirror or glass has been

etched, the lights will shine through, but

only where the mirror has been etched

will the beauty of your artwork literally

shines through whether you use white or

colored lights.

It also depends on whether you added

stained glass paint to the etching to

decide what color of light would be best

suited for your artwork.

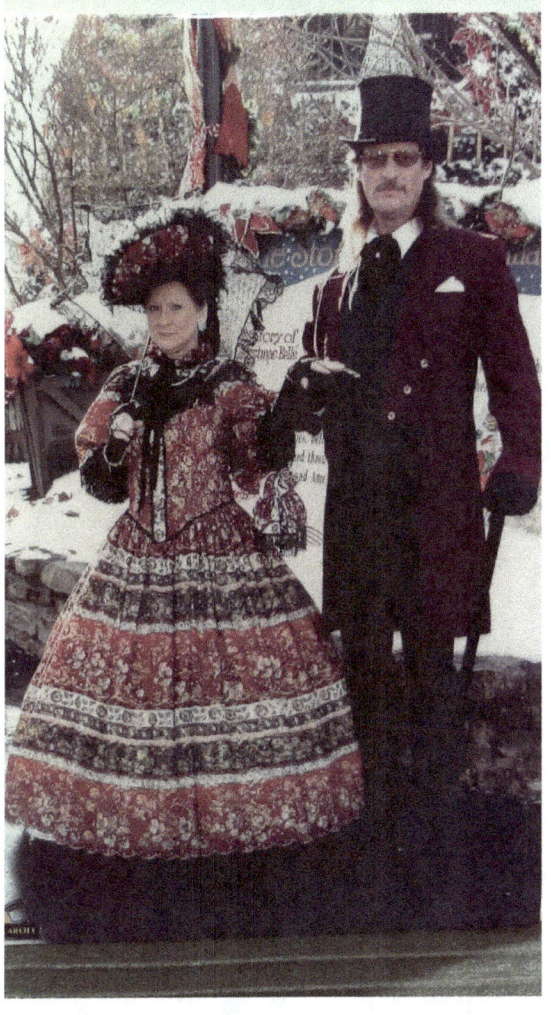

My name is Bruce W Brewer and my beautiful wife Bonita, I have been blessed with the gift of drawing: (pencil, ink, etching, painting, charcoal, and wood

carving).

I have spent my life of 60+ years, striving

to get better and be better as I go. Back

in 2010, I was in a bad accident that kept

me in a hospital for several days, and then

in and out of therapy for 4 months.

I was laid up at my brother's house

which was approximately 600 miles from

my wife, little girl (standard teacup

chihuahua) Babette, and my home.

Life has a way of picking you up and

letting you down, but the truth is, it is a

mindset.

You must learn how to control life in a

way that is more manageable, and I

found the way-out of reality for a short

time period, by taking the time to do what

I enjoy doing not because I have to, but

because I want to.

My youngest brother showed me what to

do and what I needed to do, but it was up

to me to figure out the way I felt most

comfortable with. This part of the

artwork world is considered trial and

error.

My first attempt was to freehand the

Harley Davidson banner onto the back of

a mirror, etch it out and my brother will

display it in his house.

I forgot that if you do not turn the letters

backward, when I turned the mirror

around, all the words were backward.

I thought I would fail (first attempt in

learning), but my brother said it was

awesome, so he framed it and placed it

on the wall in his restroom on the

opposite side of the mirror he used to

shave with.

Now he can look at the mirror the way it

was supposed to have turned out

originally.

Artwork has always been my passion

and I have a calming and relaxing way

about it. Your artwork will never be

perfect for you but others will not

recognize anything wrong unless you

point it out.

Be proud of what you have done and

remember there is no such thing as

being a perfectionist because nothing

will ever be perfect, but it will be the best

that You can do, and the more you do it

the better you will get at it.

This is my first attempt at writing about

something that I have enjoyed doing,

Having trial and error with the problem

of breaking a few mirrors because I

etched too deep into the glass, or set the

mirror on the floor so I could get myself

something to drink, and accidentally

rolled my chair into the mirror and

busted it into many pieces.

This was before I learned to place some

kind of shelving adhesive or even clear

wide tape on the mirror side of the

mirror, so, whenever the glass might

crack or break, it would not send shards

of broken glass everywhere.

The clear adhesive tape or shelf liner will

allow you to see what your artwork

looks like when you turn the mirror

around so you can see what was etched.

Not if but when you break one of your

masterpieces, you just do it again.

This is a learning experience, it is not like

it is not going to happen, but when will it

happen?

Do not get upset because it happens to

everyone at one point or another when

you etch mirrors.

It seems that when this happens, it will

make you more aware of how deep you

etch the glass, be aware of where you

place the mirror, and try to keep it from

happening again.

After this type of incident(s) happened,

the next etching seemed to be a better

piece of artwork than the one before, it is

because now you want to make sure this

does not happen again, soon.

This process is a comforting way to

embrace the talent deep inside of you.

This is my first book and would like to

teach others how I have learned to enjoy

what keeps me calm and pay it forward

because of my youngest brother Vincent

(RIP). Stay focused, and be in your

moment of relaxation from the world

around you.

Do what you like doing best, and show

your skills in a way no one would ever

dream of.

This is my artist getaway for expression

and displayed for everyone to see and

appreciate.

The more you practice etching glass or

mirrors, the more exciting you get and

the More of the artwork, you will show

others.

This is the beauty and artistic ability

others will see, this will start others

talking and bragging about such

beautiful works of art you have

produced.

When they start talking to family and

friends about what they have witnessed

with their own eyes. They will have

others wanting to know more, and

before long, you might have a side income

that will help pay for more material, pay a

bill, by gas or whatever you like, as you

learn a new skill and enjoy what is

relaxing, rewarding and it will place

you in a happier state of mind.

This book has been written to help guide

the beginner and to give them some

understanding of what is possible and to

have fun and learn a new skill.

From an artist, author, life coach &

mentor, to another artist.

I want to express my most inward

concern for your safety from me to you,

please be aware of the safety hazards

involved and be patient.

Your innermost talent that you have

been blessed with will help you enjoy and

have Fun with this new and exciting way

of art that you are going to create.

But please protect yourself, and the

room around you. Thank you for your

time and interest. **You can do this!!!**

https://facebook.com/bruce.brewer